Literature-based Theme Unit

We Are All Stars!

Educational Materials by
Mary Lou Datema and
Dr. Brenda Bradshaw

Infinity Kids Press
Springfield, Missouri
www.infinitykidspress.com

Literature-Based Theme Unit: We Are All Stars!

Copyright © Mary Lou Datema and Dr. Brenda Bradshaw
First Edition, Goldminds Publishing, LLC, March 2016
Second Edition, Infinity Kids Press, February 2021

ISBN 13: 978-0-9994098-7-9

PUBLISHER'S NOTE: Without limiting the rights under the copyright reserved above, no part of this publication may be reproduced, stored in or introduced into a retrieval system, or transmitted, in any form or by any means (electronic, mechanical, photocopying, recording or otherwise), without the prior written permission of both the copyright owner and the above publisher of this book.

Infinity Kids Press
Springfield, Missouri
www.infinitykidspress.com

Printed in the United States of America

Table of Contents

Introduction	1
Assistive Devices	4
Less Visible Needs	6
We All Have Needs	7
Role-play Games	8
My Community	15
Therapy Pets	17
Always Be Kind	20
Help Arlo (Maze)	21
Matching	22
Parent Letter	23

Copyright 2016, Datema & Bradshaw

Introduction

Synopsis
Young children are invited to visit a rollicking and welcoming, inclusive classroom where children of differing abilities learn and play together every day. Come join the fun!

Objectives for Reading *We Are All Stars!*
1. To provide young children with exposure to a variety of disabilities and related equipment
2. To support the idea that we are all good at something and, at the same time, we are all learning something
3. To provide a format that enables young children to discuss and ask questions about disabilities in a supportive and informative setting
4. To increase acceptance of diverse populations and to encourage appropriate social skills with all students

Children often have questions when they see a person who is differently-abled……because asking questions is how children learn. Adults are sometimes uncomfortable answering these questions because many of us we were raised not to talk about, notice or comment on anything out of the ordinary with another person. Children ask questions about people with disabilities not to be cruel or unkind, but because they are really seeking information. It's our job as adults to make sure children have the information they need to understand a diverse individual.

It's also important that young children learn to see those with disabilities as equals, not as objects of pity. Keep stressing that we are all good at something, some things are hard for us, and we are all learning to do new things all the time- they just might be different things. For some children, it might be learning to write their name or count to 20. For some children, it might be learning to walk independently or talk. For some, it might be learning to navigate with a wheelchair or a cane. We all help each other learn and grow.

Vocabulary to Think About Before Reading the Book to Children

Acceptance -

Disability -

Diversity -

Friends -

Kindness -

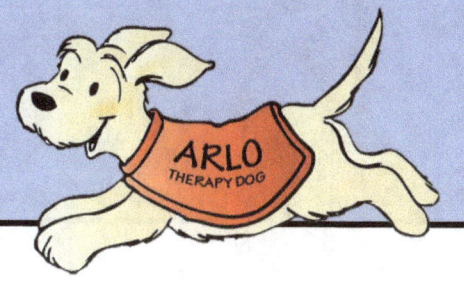

Introduction

Special-education Vocabulary to be Familiar with Before Reading the Book to Children

Autism (Brody) - Autism is a lifelong developmental disability characterized by disturbances in communication, sensory processing and social skills. Autism falls along a range from mild to more severe, so it is termed a "spectrum disorder."

Anxiety (Kylie) - An emotion characterized by feelings of tension or worry.

AFO's (Ryan) - A brace worn to support the ankle and foot.

Blind/visually impaired (Ashley) - The inability to see; a severe reduction in vision that can't be significantly corrected with surgery, glasses or contact lenses.

Cochlear implant (Gracie) - A device that can be surgically implanted in the cochlea to stimulate it to cause a sensation of sound to those that are severely hearing impaired or deaf.

Deaf/hearing impaired (Gracie) - The inability to hear; the loss of functional hearing.

Picture communication (Aiden) - Any system by which a person who is non-verbal uses pictures to communicate with others and gets wants and needs met.

Therapy dog (Arlo) - A dog that is specially trained to provide support and comfort to people.

Stander (Bennett) - A device that allows people with little core or leg strength to stand for a time.

Walker (Greta) - A framework designed to support someone who has difficulty walking.

Wheelchair (Lilliann) - A special wheeled chair to help those who can't walk by themselves gain mobility.

White cane (Ashley) - The cane commonly used by visually impaired people to navigate their environment.

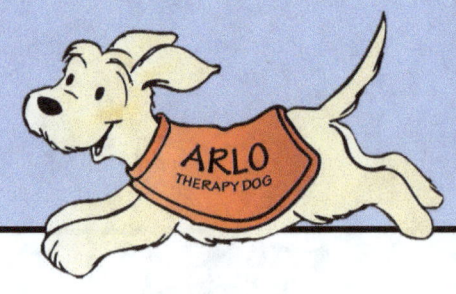

Introduction

Less Visible Special Needs

Sometimes, people have needs that don't require equipment or special devices, but their needs do require us to be kind and understanding. Their needs may not be as easy to see. Remember, everybody is learning something, whether identified with special needs or not, and whether their individual needs and concerns are easily visible or not.

Anxiety (Kylie) – A feeling of nervousness or shyness when doing something new.

Chronic illness (Casey) – Being sick a lot, resulting in numerous absences from school. The teacher or school nurse also works to keep the student healthy at school.

Sensory processing disorder (Justin) – Difficulty with processing sensory input, such as dislike for touching sticky or messy things, discomfort with certain sounds, sensitivity to certain types of light, taste or texture issues with eating, sensitivity to certain smells.

Fine motor issues (Samuel) – Difficulty with fine motor tasks such as writing, cutting or drawing.

For more information about talking to young children about disabilities:
https://www.care.com/a/teaching-your-child-about-peers-with-special-needs-0812040913

Copyright 2016, Datema & Bradshaw

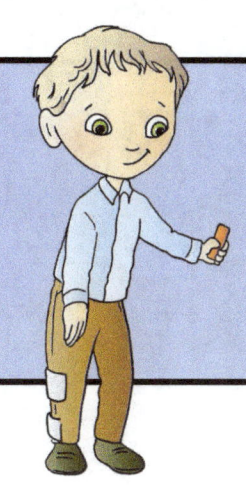

Assistive Devices

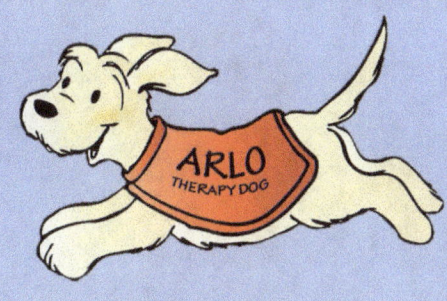

Class discussion: We all use devices to help us every day. Here are some examples. How does each device help us?

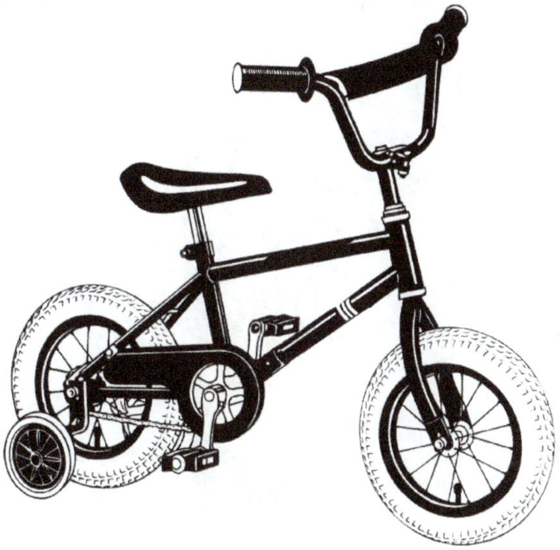

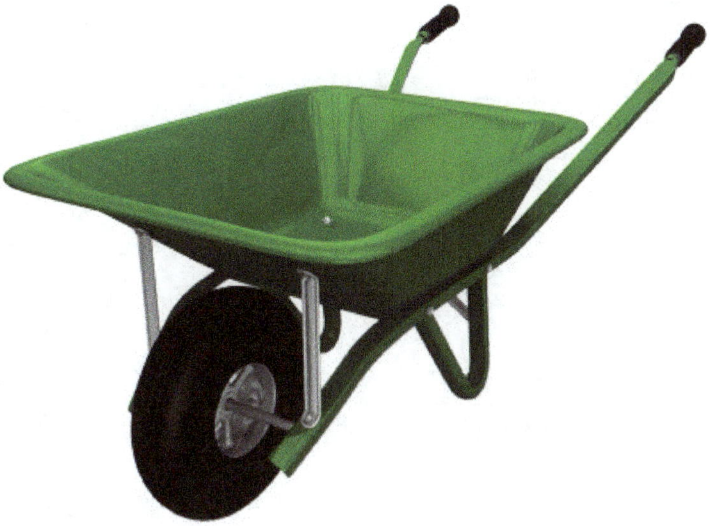

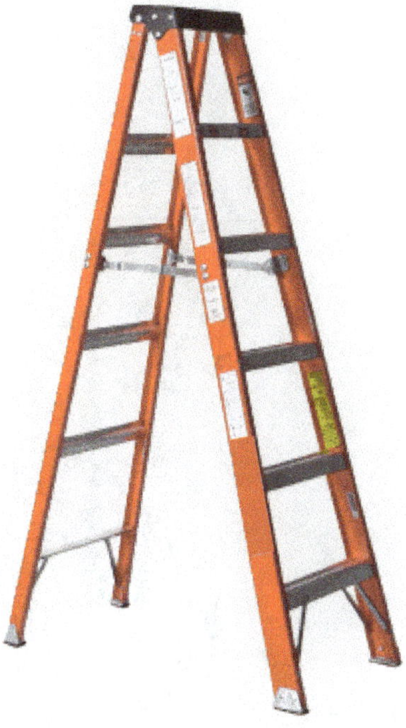

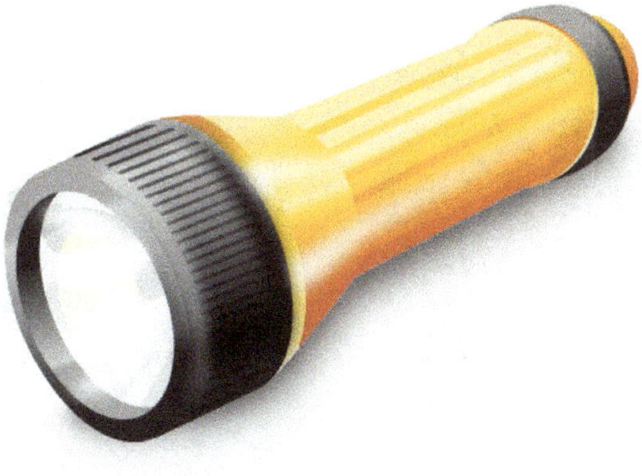

Copyright 2016, Datema & Bradshaw

Assistive Devices

Class discussion: Some people have special or different needs and use devices to help them. These devices may look different than the things most people use every day, but the idea is the same. Can you find them in the story? How do they help the character?

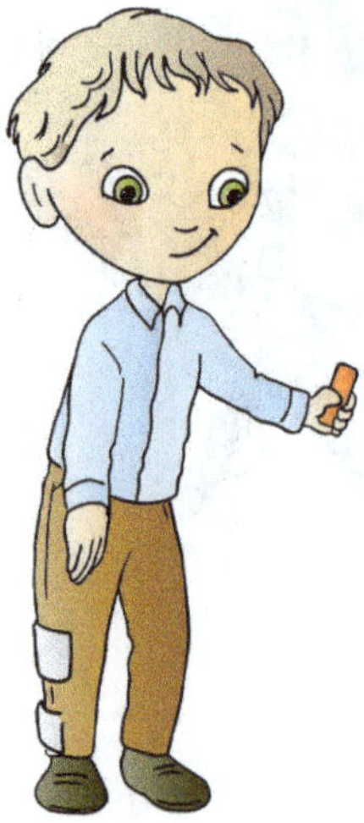

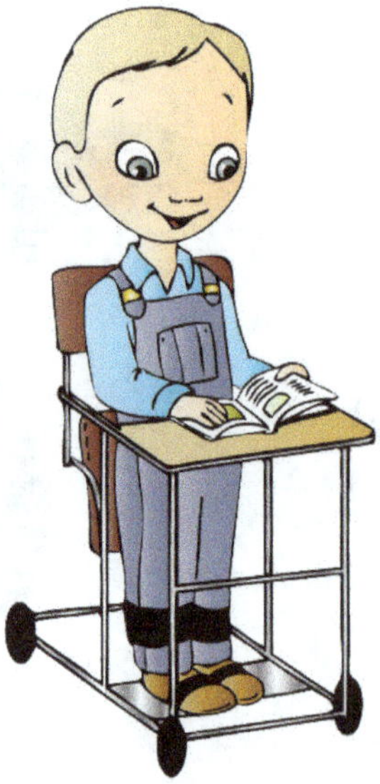

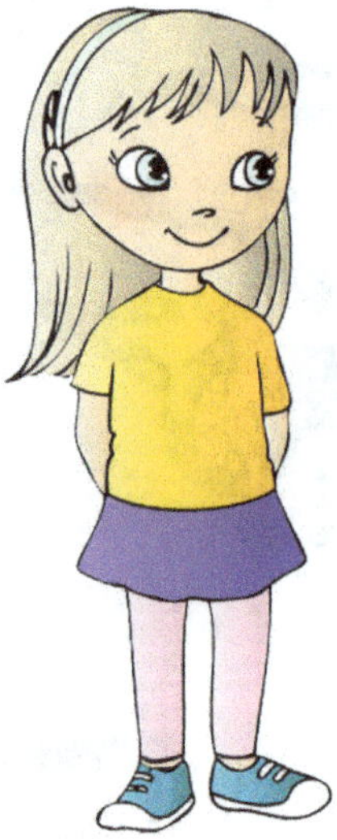

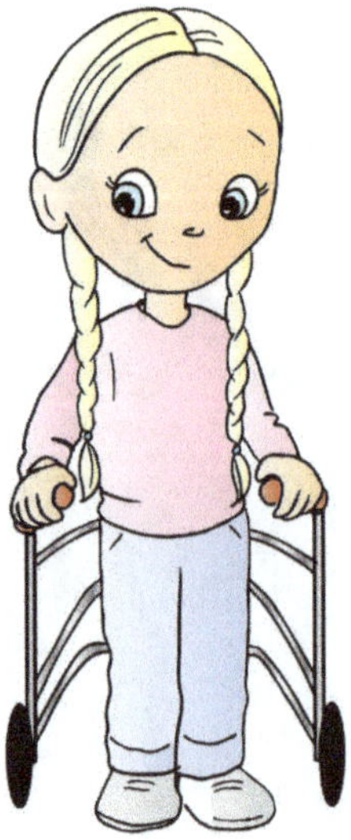

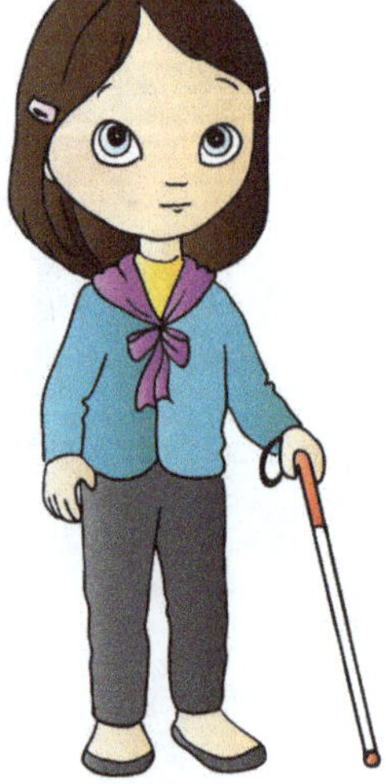

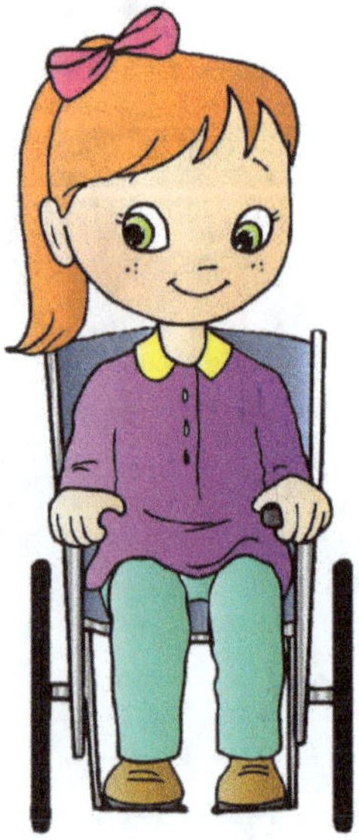

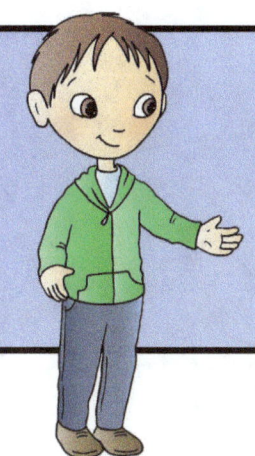

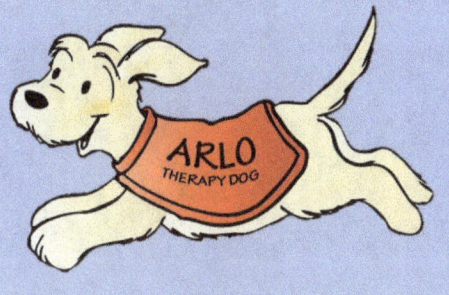

Less Visible Needs

Class discussion: Some people have different needs that don't require special equipment or devices. Their special needs may not be as easy to see, but they need us to be kind and understanding. Can you find these characters in the book? How can we show kindness to others with these needs?

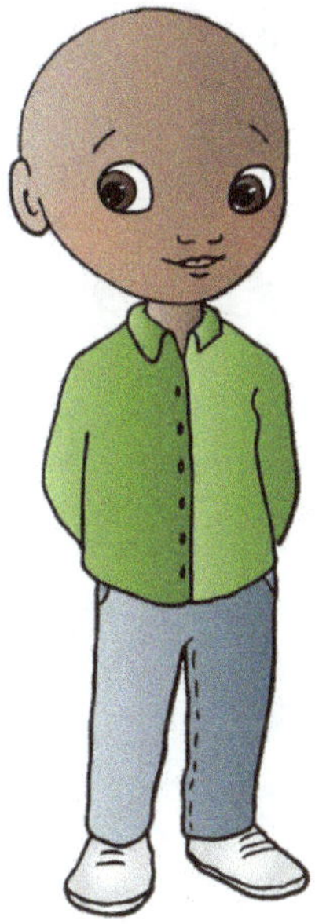
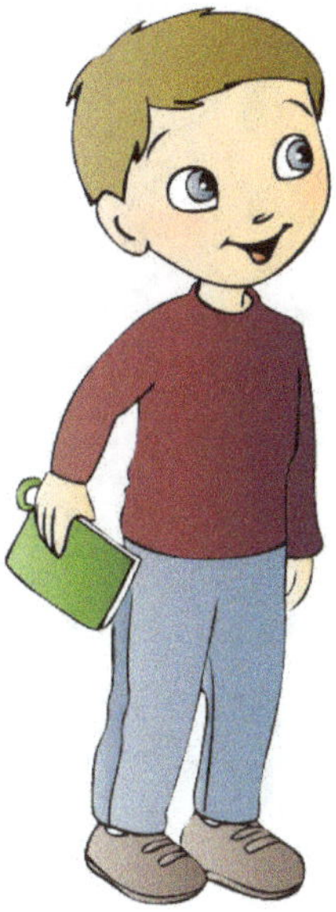
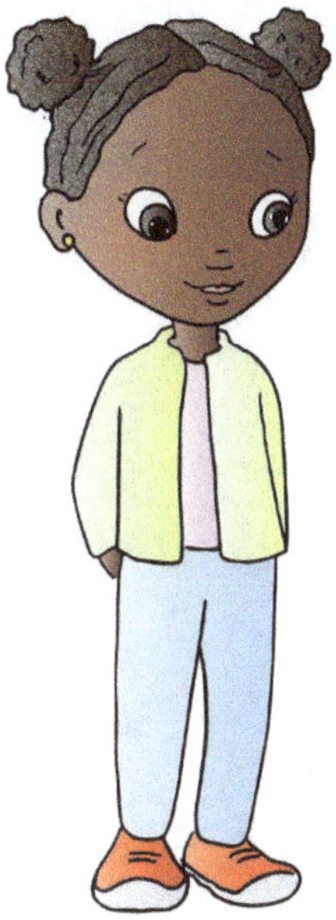
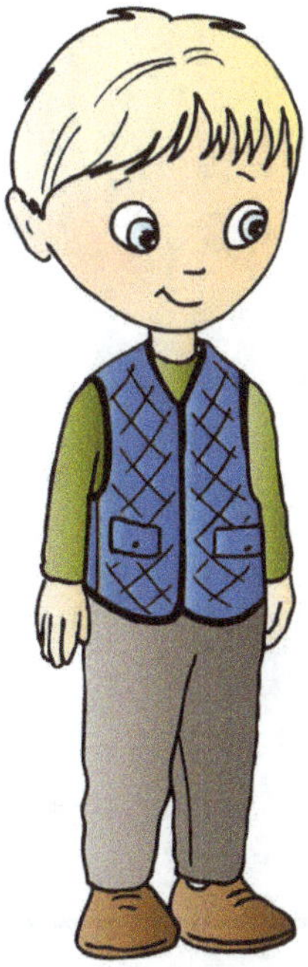
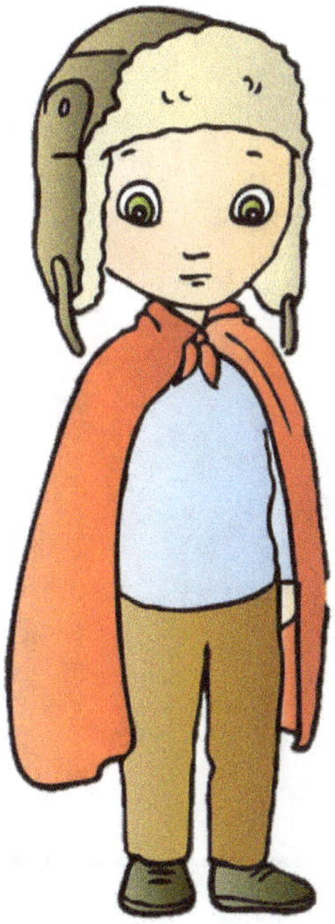

Copyright 2016, Datema & Bradshaw

We All Have Needs

Draw a picture of yourself doing something you need help with every day. You can use a device for help, or get help from another person.

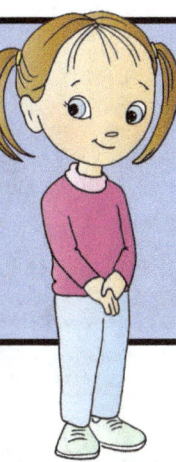

Role-play Games

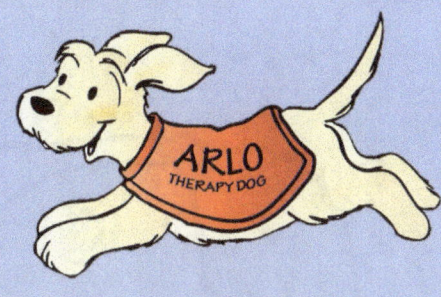

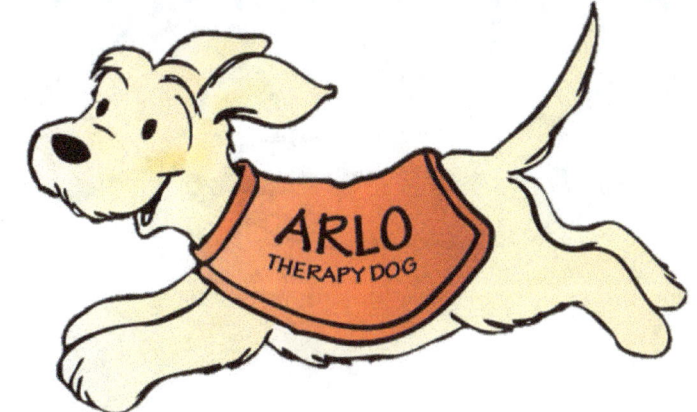

The accompanying images of characters from the book can easily be cut out and made into stick puppets or puppets that stand using binder clips. Using puppets is a great way to act out various situations in the classroom, teach social skills such as how to be kind to others and work on socially appropriate questions and language. Children can role play specific situations involving being kind and helpful using the puppets.

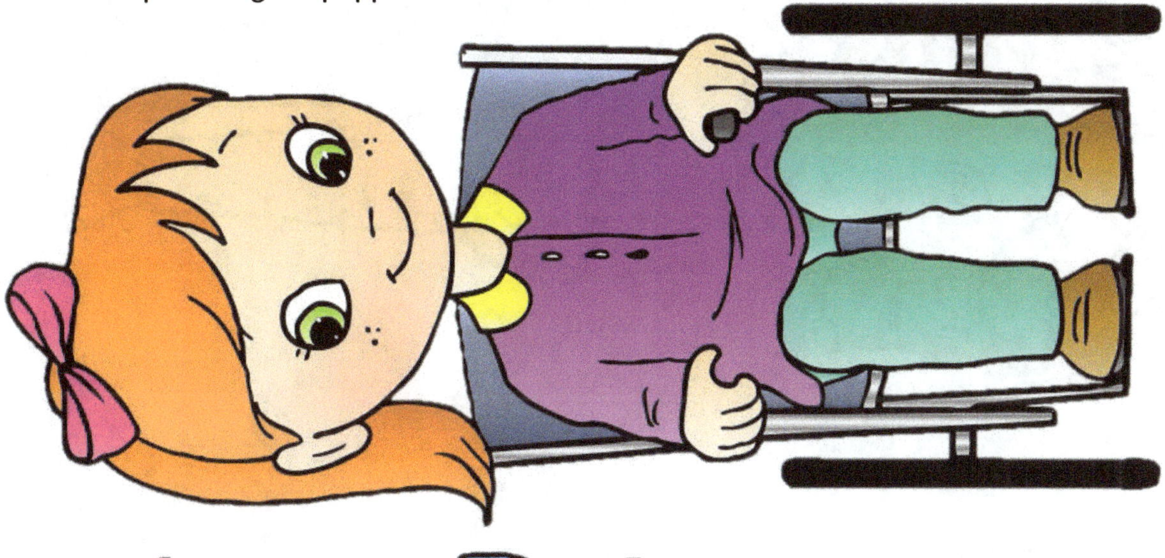

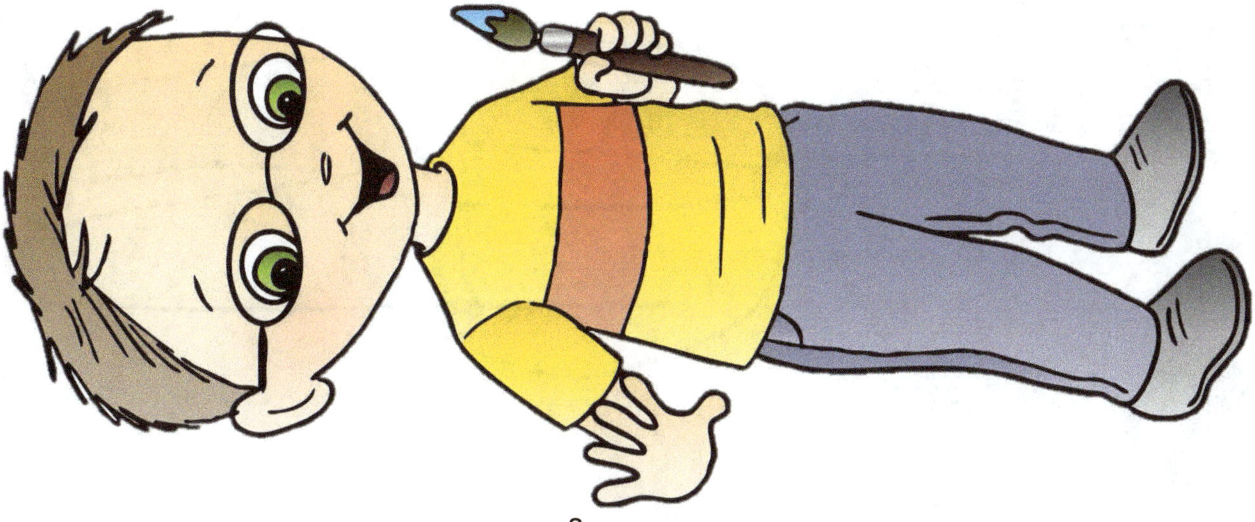

Copyright 2016, Datema & Bradshaw

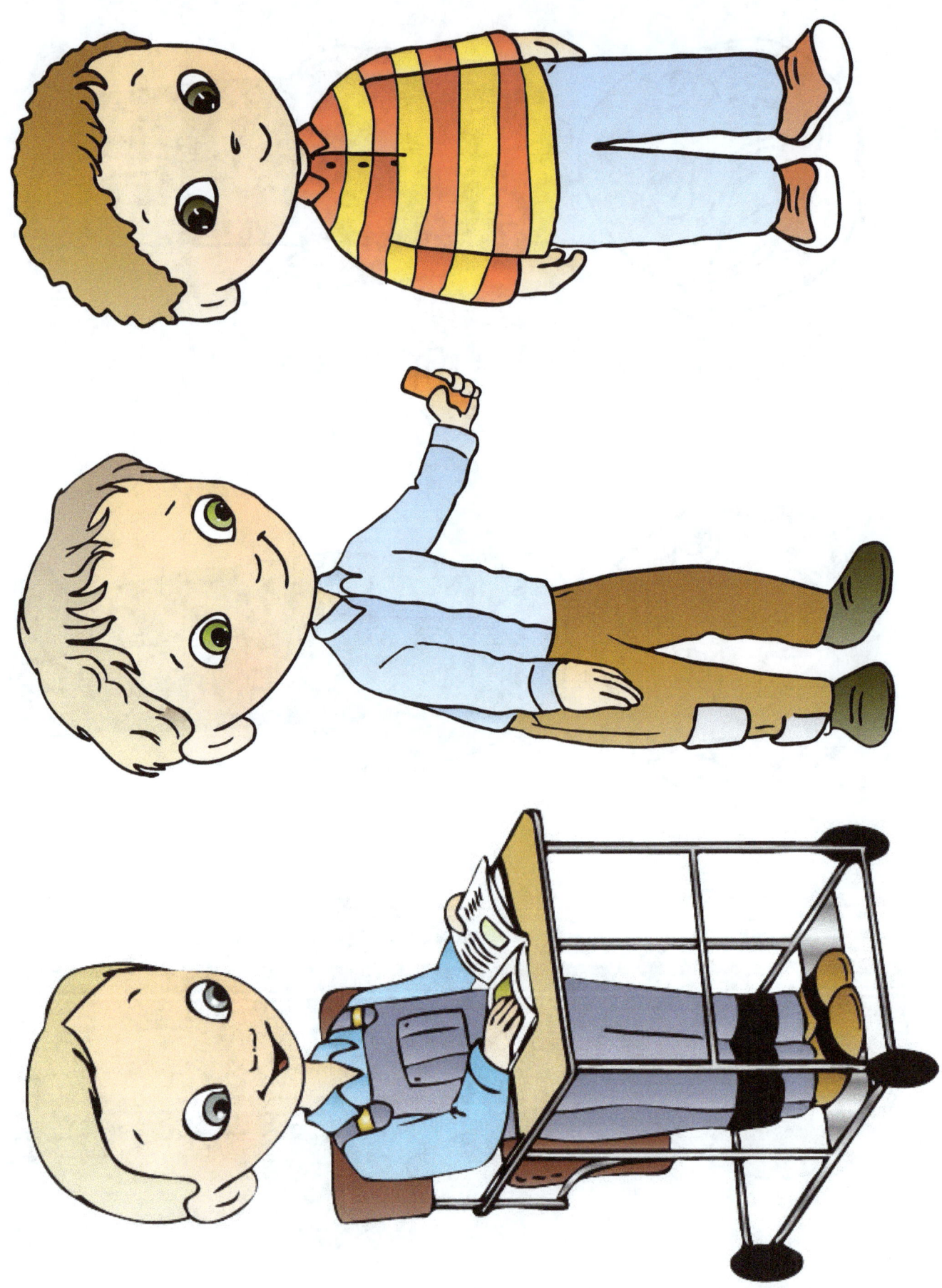

 # My Community

Community-building reinforces the idea that every child in your classroom is a valued member of the school community. Building opportunities for cooperation and collaboration into your day helps to reinforce this as your encourage children to work together. Here are some great community building ideas that encourage working together and acknowledgement of all:

Start your day with some group activities that build community- a song that greets everybody, includes handshakes or high fives for all, uses each student's name or recognizes and welcomes every student in some way. This is a great morning routine. It also shows your little ones that you are setting the expectation that everybody is recognized as an important member of the community.

- A large piece of paper on an interior or exterior wall-children work together with art materials to create a beautiful collage

- Building materials that children can share to make a sculpture or structure together, such as cardboard pieces, wallpaper scraps, toilet paper or paper towel rolls, almost anything out of the recycle bin!

- Building with marshmallows and toothpicks or, for younger children, marshmallows and drinking straws. How tall can you build a structure? How can you help each other?

- Intentionally plan activities where children are encouraged to share materials, engage in conversation and get to know each other better. Dramatic play, block play and sensory play in a large, flat container are great for this.

- Make one bulletin board into a giant puzzle. Each child in your classroom decorates one piece. The puzzle isn't complete without everybody!

- Some schools are beginning to use buddy benches. A buddy bench is a designated place that a child can go and sit while waiting for a friend to play with. Others are encouraged to go to the bench and specifically ask that child to join in their play. Teacher your children how to use the buddy bench and nobody is ever left out!

- Show the children the book cover (front and back). Ask, "How do you know this is a happy community?" Discuss aspects of the picture like the smiles, everyone is included, there are choices of many things to do, etc.

- Use the image on the next page to find things in the classroom community (and also work on listening skills). For example, ask students to put an "X" on the student in a wheelchair, or circle the teacher.

Therapy Pets

Therapy pets have many benefits to all children:

- Improves physical health through relaxation and positive interaction, and aids the development of motor skills and speeds recovery time for illness.
- Improves mental and emotional health by providing comfort, attention, reducing boredom and decreasing feelings of isolation and loneliness.
- With improved overall health, children can focus better and greater confidence in improving academic and social skills.

Dogs tend to be the pet of choice because they are easy to train and very loyal and attentive to humans. Hypoallergenic breeds are preferred in case there are allergies to dogs in the classroom. Other class pets are also beneficial, such as guinea pigs and fish, which are entertaining and relaxing to watch.

Schools often have restrictions on the types of animals allowed in classrooms, so be sure to check with your administrator before adopting a pet or inviting a pet therapy dog to your classroom.

For more information about therapy dogs and setting up a visit at your school:
http://www.tdi-dog.org/

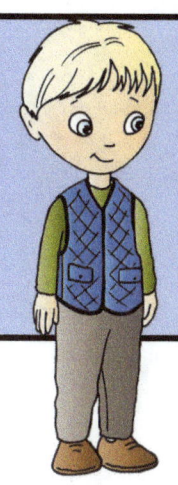

Therapy Pets

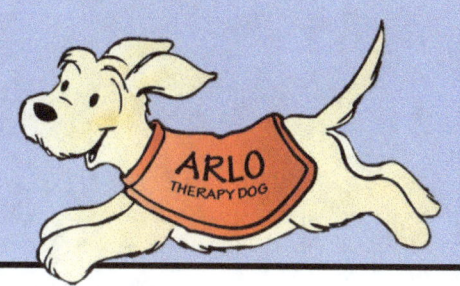

Circle the things Arlo needs.
Place an X over the things Arlo does not need.

Copyright 2016, Datema & Bradshaw

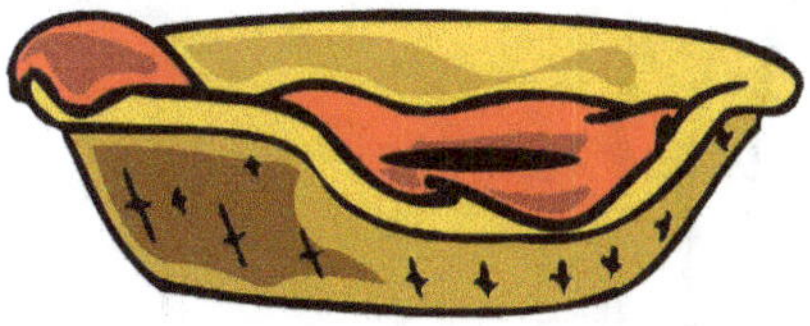

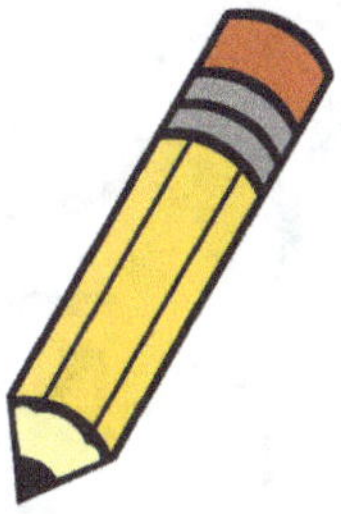

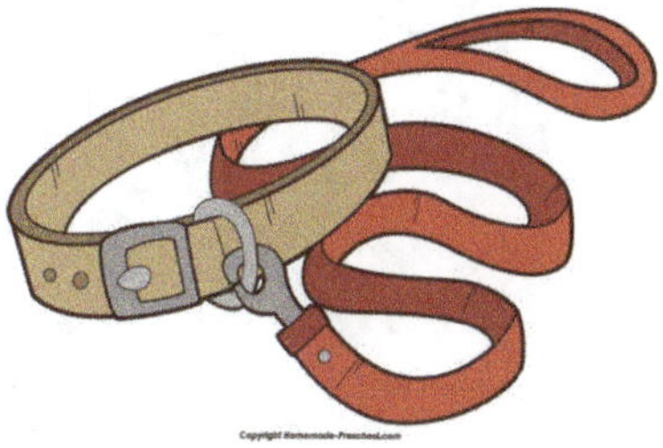

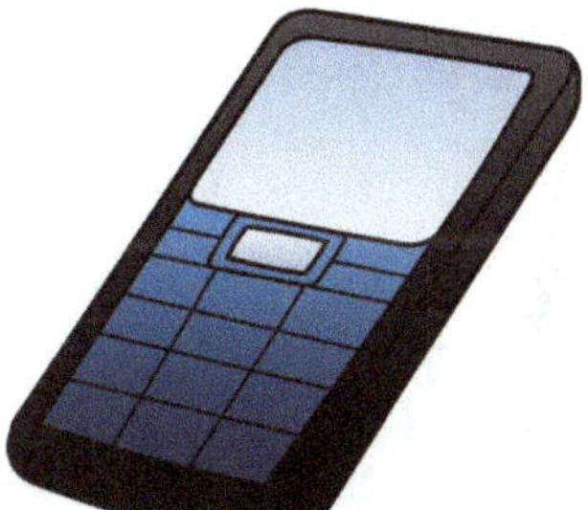

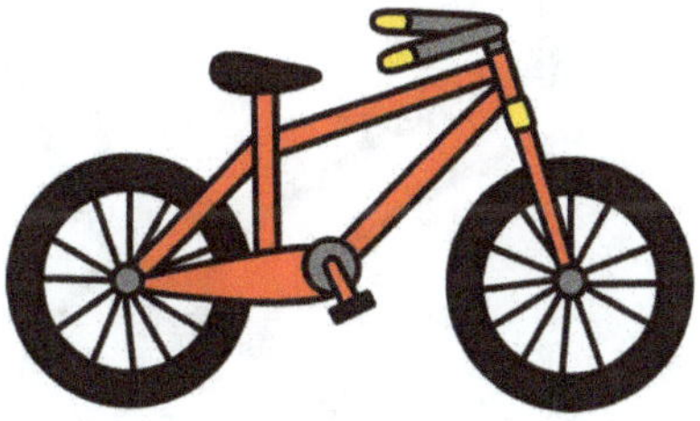

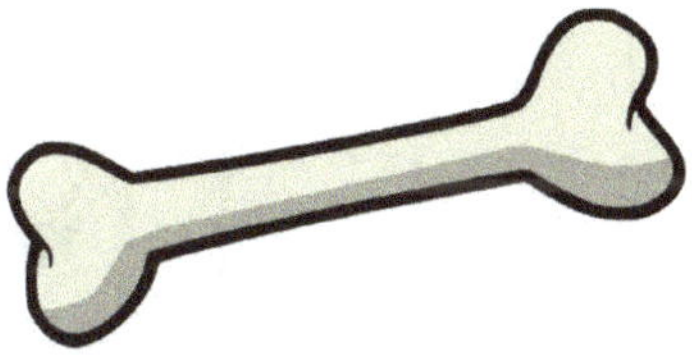

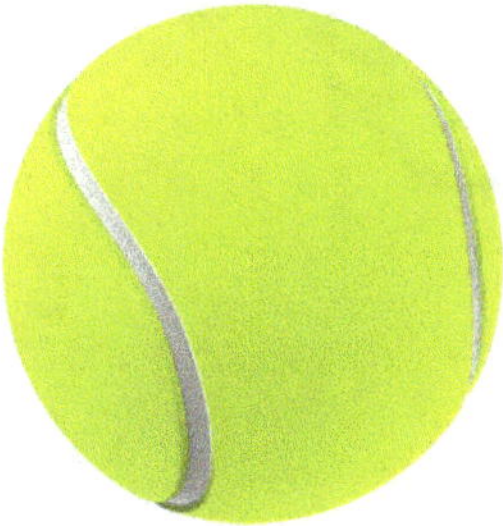

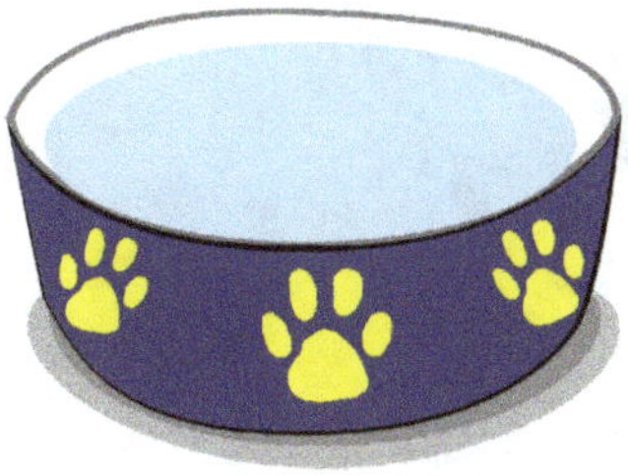

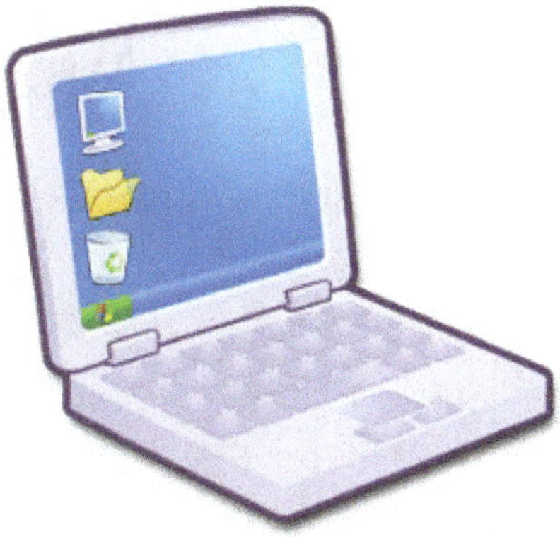

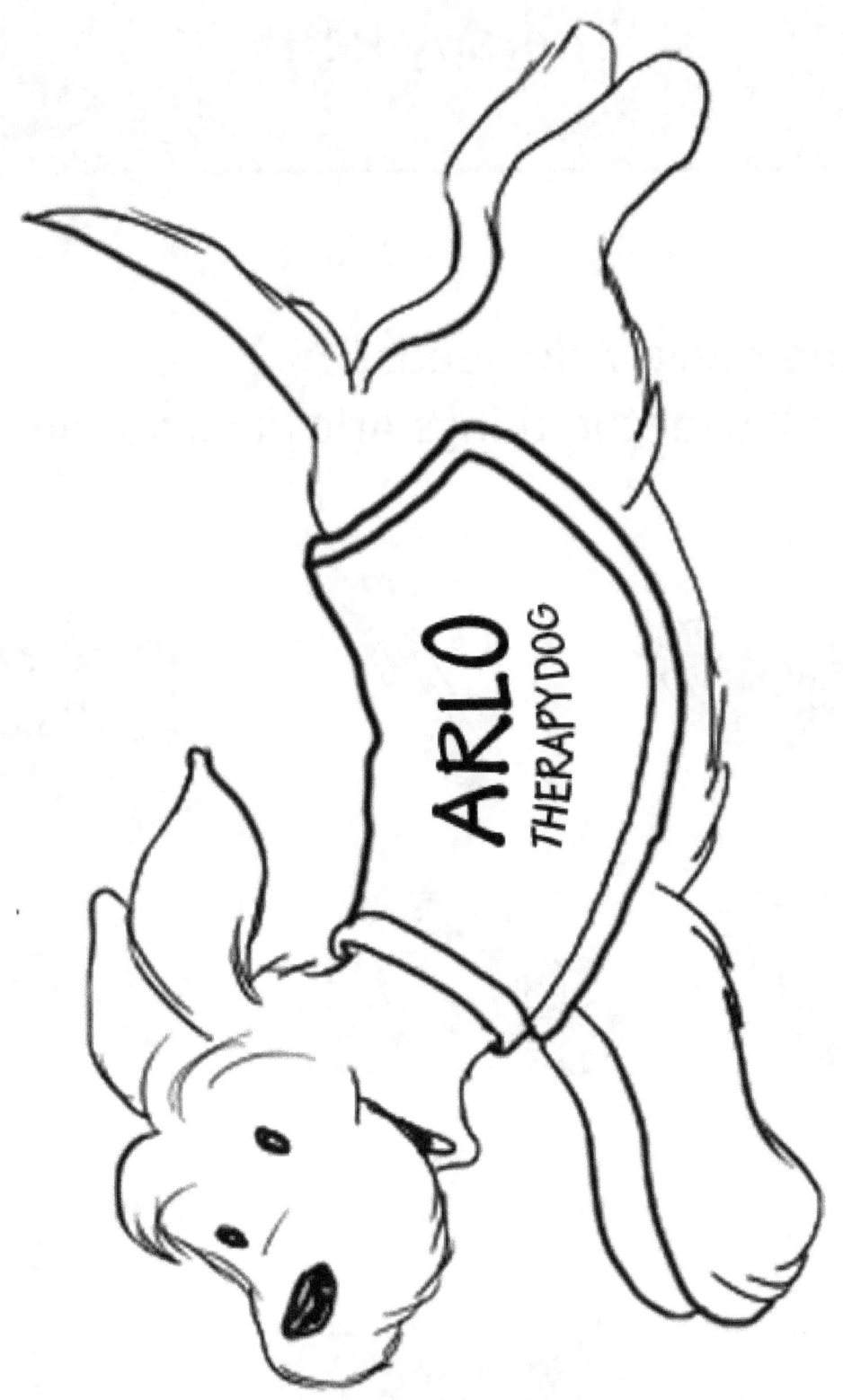

Always Be Kind

Class Discussion: Crumple up a big paper heart, and when you try to flatten it out again, you still see the crinkles, no matter what. Try to always be kind and say nice words. Even if you apologize to another person, the damage you did is still there.

Class Discussion: We may look different on the outside, but we are all the same on the inside. We all want to have friends and to be happy. Show the children several different types of eggs, different sizes, different colors. Point out that the eggs look a little different on the outside. Now, break each egg into a bowl. Point out that the eggs look much the same on the inside. The same activity can be done with different colors of M and M's also. The children can take a tiny bite of their M and M so see that, even if they look different on the outside, the insides are the same.

Copyright 2016, Datema & Bradshaw

Help Arlo

Help Arlo find his way to his friend, Casey.

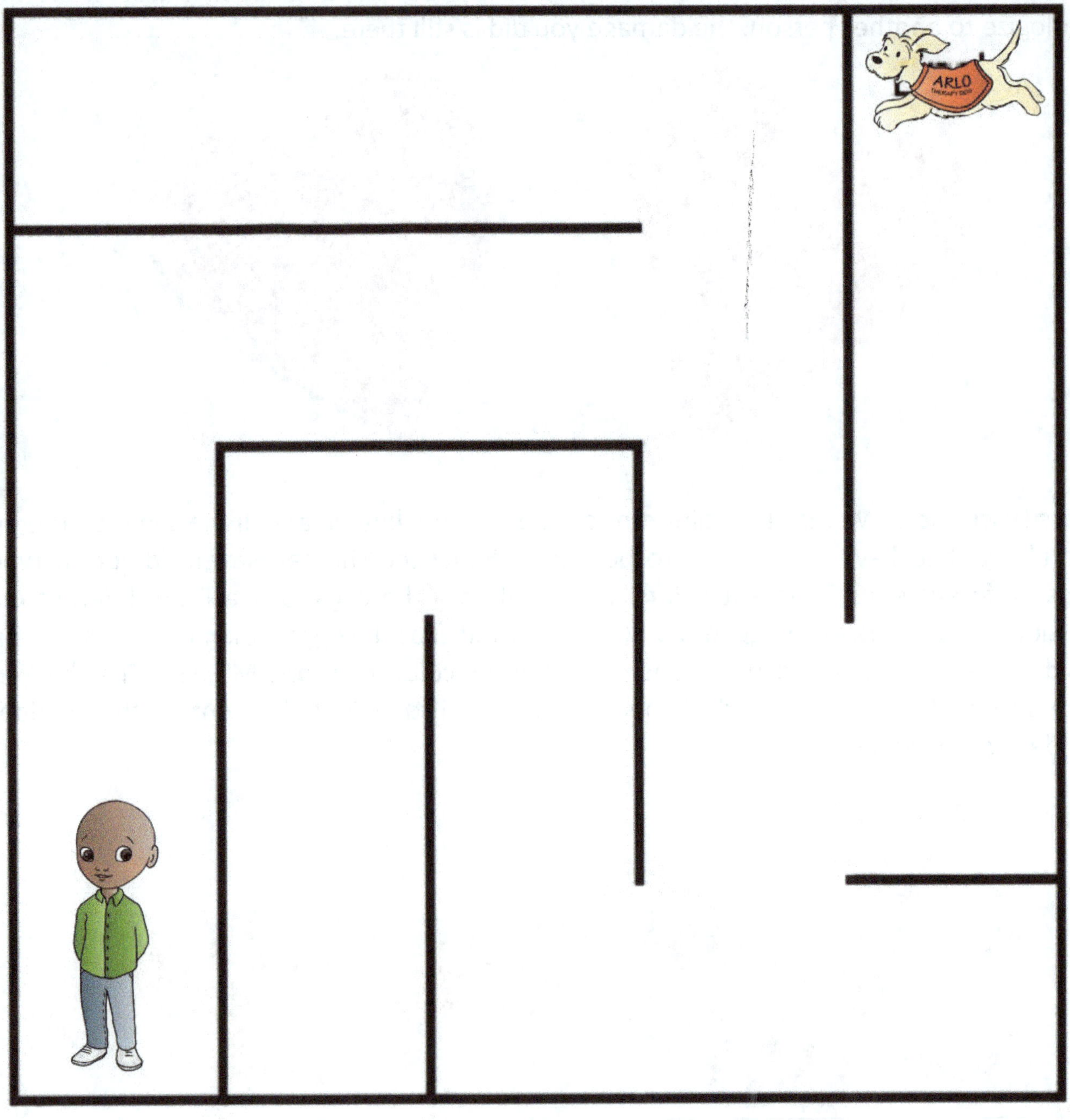

Matching
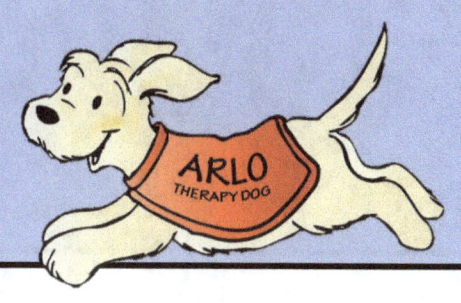

Parent Letter

Date:

Dear Parents and Guardians,

Today at school our class read the book, *We Are All Stars!* We discussed how everybody is good at something, everybody is learning something, and that we all help each other. We were able to learn about and discuss the fact that some people might even need special equipment to help them every day. We learned that it is ok to ask polite questions to learn about other people because understanding leads to acceptance.

We learned about these vocabulary words:

>   acceptance
>   disability
>   diversity
>   friends
>   kindness

We also learned about different kinds of equipment that people might use if they have a special need, and that some people even have special needs we can't "see."

We hope that by understanding individual differences we can promote acceptance of all children. You can help your child learn today's lesson by reviewing the vocabulary words and inviting ongoing discussions about different abilities. Most young children don't mean to be cruel or unkind, but it's important that they learn to ask questions about others respectfully and kindly. You can help with that at home by modeling your own acceptance and willingness to answer your child's questions.

Sincerely,

www.ingramcontent.com/pod-product-compliance
Lightning Source LLC
Chambersburg PA
CBHW060429010526
44118CB00017B/2418